NATIONS IN CONFLICT

NORTH KOREA

by PEGGY J. PARKS

BLACKBIRCH®
PRESS

San Diego • Detroit • New York • San Francisco • Cleveland • New Haven, Conn. • Waterville, Maine • London • Munich

THOMSON
★ ™
GALE

For more information, contact
The Gale Group, Inc.
27500 Drake Rd.
Farmington Hills, MI 48331-3535
Or you can visit our Internet site at http://www.gale.com

Photo credits: cover, page 15, 29, 34 © AP Wide World; page 5 (map) © Amy Stirnkorb Design; pages 6-7, 8, 9, 10, 13, 17, 18, 22, 26, 27, 37, 39, 41, 42, 43 © CORBIS; pages 20-21 © Art Resource; page 24 © NARA; page 33 © North Wind Archives

LIBRARY OF CONGRESS CATALOGING-IN-PUBLICATION DATA

Parks, Peggy.
  North Korea / By Peggy Parks.
    v. cm. — (Nations in conflict)
Includes bibliographical references and index.
Contents: A divided nation — Place, people, past — Political turmoil — An uncertain future.
  ISBN 1-4103-0077-3 (hardback : alk. paper)
  1. Korea (North)—Juvenile literature. 2. Korea (North)—Social conditions—Juvenile literature. 3. Nuclear weapons—Korea (North)—Juvenile literature. [1. Korea (North)] I. Title. II. Series.

DS932.P37 2003
951.9304'3—dc21   2002153744

Printed in United States
10 9 8 7 6 5 4 3 2 1

CONTENTS

A Divided Nation

Until about fifty years ago, there was no North Korea and South Korea. There was only Korea, a unified nation known as the Land of Morning Calm. Author Shannon McCune describes the country: "Early in the morning in Korea the air often has a special calm and freshness to it. . . . In all seasons there is a particular quality to the mornings in Korea that projects hope for a bright new day."[1]

Since 1953, when the Korean War split Korea into two countries, it has not been united. For that reason, McCune calls it the Land of Broken Calm. North Korea is now a Communist nation separated from South Korea by an area known as the demilitarized zone (DMZ), a border that is more than a mile wide and 150 miles long. All along the DMZ, armed soldiers are constantly on patrol duty—North Korean soldiers on the north side, and South Korean and American soldiers on the south side. Anyone who tries to cross the border in either direction, without the North Korean government's permission, may be captured or shot.

Ellie Kuykendall, an American teacher who lived and worked in South Korea for a year, describes the DMZ: "I expected barbed wire all along it, but much of the border has nothing to mark it. However, when you are there, you definitely know where you're allowed to stand. I was told that

even if I stepped back ten inches, I would be on North Korean property. . . .
My guide said that I probably wouldn't be shot, but that there was no
reason why they couldn't shoot me."[2]

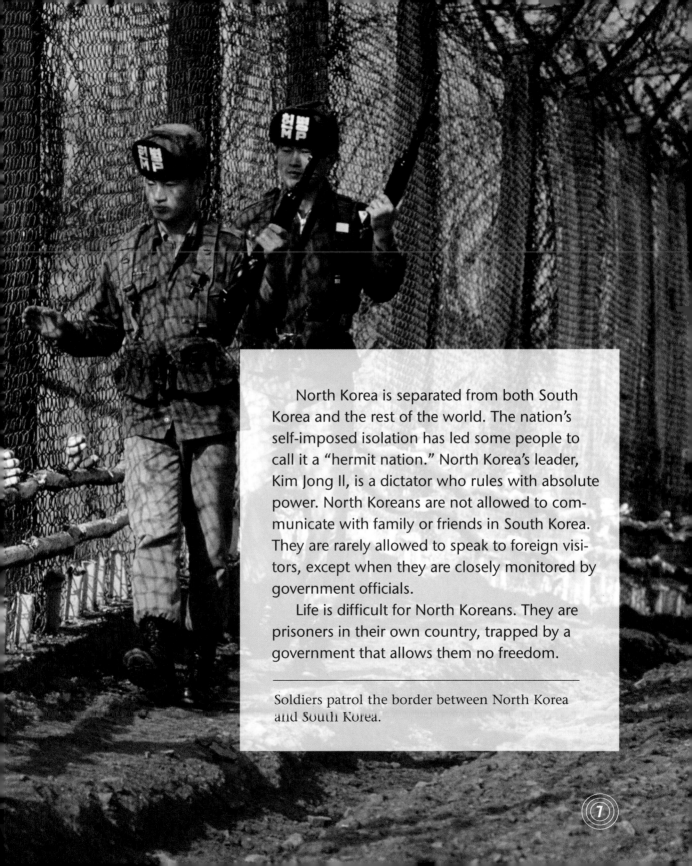

North Korea is separated from both South Korea and the rest of the world. The nation's self-imposed isolation has led some people to call it a "hermit nation." North Korea's leader, Kim Jong Il, is a dictator who rules with absolute power. North Koreans are not allowed to communicate with family or friends in South Korea. They are rarely allowed to speak to foreign visitors, except when they are closely monitored by government officials.

Life is difficult for North Koreans. They are prisoners in their own country, trapped by a government that allows them no freedom.

Soldiers patrol the border between North Korea and South Korea.

Above: Much of North Korea's farmland has been destroyed by natural disasters. This is one of many reasons why the people who live there are so poor.

Left: Many children in North Korea receive little food or health care.

They may not practice any form of religion. They are not allowed to speak out against the government—those who do may be killed or imprisoned in labor camps, which have been described by those who have seen them as filthy and inhumane.

North Korea's people also suffer from extreme poverty, a severe shortage of food, and poor health care. Since the Soviet Union's collapse in 1991, North Korea no longer receives Soviet financial aid, which paid for food, fuel, and other necessities. To make matters worse, a series of natural disasters from 1995 to 1997 destroyed nearly all of North Korea's farmland. By the end of the 1990s, hundreds of thousands of North Koreans had died from malnutrition and related conditions.

North Korea is a country whose people want nothing more than peace and freedom. They have been beaten down by tyrannical leadership, natural disasters, starvation, and disease. They are kept apart from the rest of the world. Norbert Vollertsen, a German doctor who lived and worked in North Korea, sums up the hermit nation: "I know North Korea. I have lived there, and have witnessed its hell and madness."[3]

CHAPTER ONE

Place, People, Past

On the far eastern side of the continent of Asia lies North Korea. At just under 50,000 square miles, the country is tiny when compared to China, its massive neighbor to the north. To the west, North Korea is bordered by the Yellow Sea, to the east by the Sea of Japan, and to the south by South Korea.

About 80 percent of North Korea is covered by mountains and dense forests. Most of the people live in the plains and lowland areas around the mountains. Because of the rugged terrain, only about 20 percent of the land is suitable for agriculture. Rice is an important crop, and about half the farmland is covered with rice paddies. North Korean farmers also grow barley, wheat, and corn. Other crops include soybeans, potatoes, and cotton.

Battles with Nature

North Korea's winters are long and cold, with temperatures that average below freezing from November through April. Summers tend to be short, hot, and very humid. Heavy storms are common during the summer because of monsoon winds, which blow moist air up from the Pacific Ocean and cause torrential rains.

Most of North Korea is covered by mountains and forests.

One result of the heavy summer rains is severe flooding. In July and August 1995, North Korea was hit with the worst floods Korea had experienced in one hundred years. Thousands of homes were destroyed, as were dams and bridges. Roads were washed out, and telephone and electricity lines were ruined. One of the worst effects of the floods was the destruction of farmland. Nearly all of the country's rice paddies and cornfields were washed away. When the floodwaters finally left, the topsoil went with them. Because topsoil is necessary for plants to grow, much of the farmland was permanently ruined.

North Korea had not recovered from the 1995 floods before disaster struck again. In 1996, floods caused additional loss of life and more than $1.5 billion in damage. Then, a year later, the country faced another kind of natural disaster—drought. During the summer of 1997, extremely high temperatures and a lack of rain killed rice and corn crops. Later that summer, North Korea was hit by a tidal wave that destroyed more homes and farmland.

These natural disasters were devastating. Entire villages were ruined, and thousands of people were killed or left homeless. The loss of farmland and crops also caused a severe food shortage. A U.S. congressman who visited North Korea in 1997 was stunned by the starvation that affected so many people. He described families who had to eat grass, weeds, and bark. He spoke of orphaned children who did not grow normally because they lacked nutritious food.

There were, however, factors beyond natural disasters that helped cause the food shortage. According to Norbert Vollertsen, much of the responsibility lies with the North Korean government. He says the authorities decide who should receive food and who should not, and they give preference to the military and upper class. He explains why he was forced

Kept apart by the demilitarized zone (DMZ) that separates their countries, relatives in North Korea and South Korea are unable to reunite.

to leave after he had worked in North Korea for a year and a half: "I denounced the regime for its abuse of human rights, and its failure to distribute food aid to the people who needed it most. North Korea's starvation is not the result of natural disasters. The calamity is man-made. Only the regime's overthrow will end it."[4]

North Korea's People

About 22 million people live in North Korea. They have a deep respect for their land and culture. They speak Korean, a major world language spoken in thirty countries besides North and South Korea.

Koreans place great value on family. In fact, loyalty to family and respect for elders are among the most important aspects of Korean society.

THE EFFECTS OF STARVATION

According to a report from the United Nations International Children's Fund (UNICEF), as many as 2 million people in North Korea have died of starvation since 1995. The report also states that more than half of North Korean children under five years old suffer from malnutrition—and the crisis was worse than all the 110 countries surveyed.

Malnutrition is a condition that develops when someone's body does not get enough vitamins, minerals, and other nutrients needed to function properly. Most commonly, it results from inadequate food, but it can also be caused by disease or chronic diarrhea, which washes nutrients out of the body too quickly. People who are malnourished are often extremely thin, with protruding bones. Their stomachs may be bloated from fluids that build up in the body. They bruise easily, and their skin is pale, cold, and dry. Their joints ache, their tongues may be swollen or shriveled, and their lips and mouth are cracked. Their hair is thin and pulls out easily from their scalps.

Children who are malnourished often have stunted growth, which means they are short for their age. They lack energy and have weakened immune systems, so they are susceptible to colds and more serious illnesses. If the malnutrition is severe, children can suffer permanent mental retardation.

When malnutrition continues over a period of time, it can lead to starvation. To try to resist starvation, the body breaks down its own tissue and uses it as a source of calories. As a result, body fat disappears, while internal organs and muscles waste away. The damaged organs no longer function properly, which can lead to a heart attack or stroke.

Total starvation is fatal in eight to twelve weeks. It is possible for some victims to improve, but this depends on how much damage has been done. Severe starvation can cause a permanent breakdown in the body's ability to absorb nutrients, or permanent organ damage. Even if victims are given a proper diet, it is possible that they may never recover.

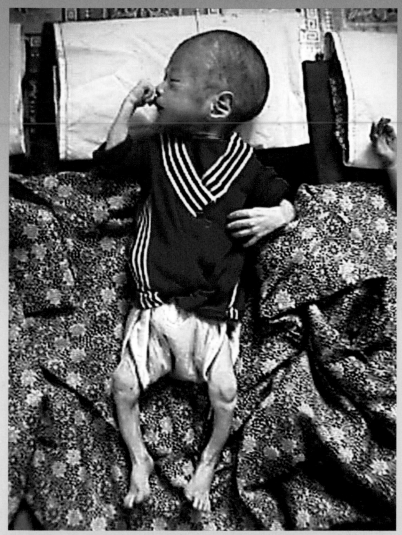

Millions of North Koreans, including children, have died of starvation since 1995.

When Korea split into two countries, families were separated. Since no one was allowed to cross the border, families had no contact with each other. Kuykendall explains how this affects them: "The people of North and South Korea hate being separated from each other. The oldest student in my class, Mr. Park, is old enough to remember when the two countries were one. . . . He said, 'I don't know if I'll ever see my uncle again. I'm getting old. He's getting old. But our two countries keep us apart.'"[5]

A Rich History

The Korean people are also proud of their history. North Korea is only fifty years old, but the history of Korea traces back thousands of years. Archaeologists have discovered ancient artifacts throughout Korea. Evidence shows that people lived there as long ago as 30,000 B.C., perhaps even earlier.

The first Koreans were probably tribal peoples who migrated from Manchuria, China, and Mongolia. Much of Korea's history is explained in legends handed down through the centuries, rather than in historical facts. According to legend, the country that is now Korea was founded in 2333 B.C. and was originally called Choson, which means "land of morning calm." Choson was founded by Tangun, a man whose father was Hwanung, the son of the creator of the universe. The legend says that Tangun's mother was a bear that had been transformed into a woman. Hwanung breathed his spirit into the woman, and she gave birth to Tangun, who later became king.

Korea's recorded history dates to 108 B.C., when the Chinese conquered Choson and established four colonies. In A.D. 313, the Chosons overthrew the Chinese and reclaimed their land. These early Koreans established the Three Kingdoms. One was called Koguryo, which was in

Pulguksa Temple was built by the Sillas in the mid-700s. It is considered a national treasure.

the north where the city of Pyongyang, North Korea's capital, is located today. The other two kingdoms were Paekche and Silla, which divided the southern coastal plains. The Three Kingdoms competed fiercely with each other, but Silla was the most powerful. In 668, with Chinese support, the Sillas conquered the other two kingdoms and unified Korea as one country.

A Time of Culture and Conflict

The Silla period marked the beginning of cultural development in Korea. The country began to prosper, and developed its own customs and language. Art, science, and literature flourished. Buddhism, which had been introduced in the fourth century, became the official religion. The Sillas built many beautiful Buddhist temples and shrines, including Pulguksa Temple and the Sokkuram Grotto, which are considered

Ch'amsongdae Observatory in Kyongju, South Korea, is the oldest astronomical observatory in the world.

national treasures. The oldest astronomical observatory in the world was built in Kyongju, the ancient Silla capital.

The Silla period was a time of great culture, but it was also a time of conflict, as different factions fought for power. In 935, a general named Wang Kon led a nonviolent revolt and seized control from the Sillas. He renamed the nation Koryo, a word that later evolved into the name Korea.

During the Koryo period, Buddhism spread throughout the country, and art and literature continued to thrive. Like the kingdoms before it, however, Koryo faced tribal uprisings. The country was also invaded by outsiders, including Japanese pirates and tribes from Mongolia and Manchuria. In 1231, Mongol forces invaded Korea. This began a war that raged on and off for nearly 30 years. Finally, Korea's king surrendered to the Mongols. Under their control, members of the royal family reigned for the next 150 years. In 1392, a Korean general named Yi Song-gye joined forces with the Ming Dynasty, which had replaced the Mongols in China. With Chinese support, he took control of Korea.

The Choson Dynasty

After Yi and his family were in power, they moved the capital to Hanyang, which is Seoul, South Korea, today. Yi's group was known as the Choson Dynasty (also called the Yi Dynasty). Korea remained under Chinese influence during this time, but for the most part, the country was independent. The Choson Dynasty leaders promoted loyalty to country and respect for parents, beliefs based on the teachings of the Chinese philosopher Confucius. Confucianism was more a philosophy than a religion, but it became so important that many people embraced it as a religion. Buddhism, however, continued to be practiced as well.

During the Choson Dynasty, invasions by external forces continued. Between 1592 and 1636, the Japanese and Manchurians attempted to invade Korea several times. They were always driven back by the Chinese-backed Choson Dynasty, but they still inflicted great damage. Thousands of Koreans died, and many towns were destroyed throughout the years of conflict.

After decades of invasions, Korea's leaders wanted to shelter the country from further attacks. In the early 1800s, they closed Korea to all non-Chinese foreigners and generally kept the borders sealed. This earned the country its nickname, hermit nation. Korea's isolation continued until 1876, when Japan sent warships to forcibly open the country to trade. To offset Japanese influence, Korea also established trade agreements with the United States and European countries.

Japanese Conquest

By the late 1800s, Japan had grown in power. In 1895, Japan and China fought the Sino-Japanese War over Korea. Japan defeated China, and then, in 1905, it defeated Russia in the Russo-Japanese War. Through these victories, Japan won a position as a world power and as Asia's lead-

ing nation. It was now strong enough to take control of Korea. In 1910, Japan removed the Choson Dynasty from power and made Korea a Japanese colony.

For the next 35 years, Japan ruled Korea and drastically changed the country. Some changes were positive, such as the modern industries and new railroads that were built. Most changes, however, were far from beneficial. Japan's rule was harsh and deprived Koreans of their freedom. To make Korean culture more like Japan's, the Japanese tried to eliminate the Korean national identity. Japanese authorities seized farmland, destroyed temples and palaces, and burned thousands of books on Korean history and geography. They declared Korean newspapers illegal, kept children out of school, and even forbade Koreans to speak their own language.

On March 1, 1919, a national Korean independence protest took place. Two million people participated in a demonstration that became

This illustration shows a battle from the Sino-Japanese War, fought in 1895.

known as the March First Movement. At the gathering, a Korean Declaration of Independence was signed. The Japanese response was immediate and brutal. More than seven thousand Koreans were killed, and thousands more were wounded or imprisoned. In spite of the Koreans' effort to achieve freedom, Japan remained in control.

CHAPTER TWO

Political Turmoil

In 1943, the world was embroiled in World War II. That year, a conference that involved the United States, Great Britain, and China was held in Cairo, Egypt. The three countries met to plan military operations against Japan, their mutual enemy. They vowed to free all nations that had been captured by Japan, including Korea, and they signed an agreement called the Cairo Declaration. This document promised freedom to Korea: "The . . . three great powers, mindful of the enslavement of the people of Korea, are determined that in due course Korea shall become free and independent."[6]

World War II ended in 1945 after Japan surrendered. The end of the war meant that Japan gave up Korea. The country was finally free from the oppressive rulers who had controlled it for more than three decades.

A Country Divided

Korea's problems were not over, however. During the final weeks of World War II, the Soviet Union had declared war on Japan and sent thousands of troops into northern Korea. After the war ended, the Soviet troops remained there. This alarmed the United States, which feared that

Koreans protested the Soviet occupation of their country at the end of World War II.

Soldiers pose with an antitank gun in South Korea. North Korea launched a surprise attack against South Korea in June 1950.

the Soviets intended to take over Korea and spread communism, a political system in which the government owns all property and strictly controls the people's lives. To prevent this, the United States sent troops to occupy the southern half of Korea. The country was divided into northern and southern sections by an invisible line known as the 38th parallel.

This division of Korea was supposed to be temporary. It was to last only until the United States, Great Britain, the Soviet Union, and China could establish a government for Korea. Over the next two years, representatives from the four nations met several times to discuss Korea's future. In 1947, the United Nations (UN) agreed to supervise countrywide elections for a new government, but the Soviets denied UN representatives access to North Korea. Elections were held in the south, however, and in 1948, Syngman Rhee was elected president of the Republic of Korea (South Korea). Later that year, the Communist-controlled government in North Korea proclaimed the independence of the Democratic People's Republic of Korea (North Korea), and Kim Il Sung became president. Korea was formally divided into two separate countries.

The Korean War

North Korea's new president was a former soldier who had spent the last years of World War II in Soviet training camps. Kim had many goals for the nation he now controlled. His first goal was to reunite North and South Korea. After that, he planned to make Korea a Communist country and become its president.

In June 1950, with the Soviet Union's support, Kim launched an invasion of South Korea. The attack was a surprise to the South Koreans, and northern forces were able to capture the capital city of Seoul. The United States, Great Britain, and fourteen other UN countries intervened on South Korea's behalf. China, a fellow Communist country, supported North Korea.

The Korean War lasted for three years. By the time it was over, nearly 3 million people—both civilians and soldiers—were dead, wounded, or missing. Another 5 million Koreans became refugees after their homes were destroyed. In July 1953, an armistice ended the fighting, but it was only a cease-fire agreement, not a peace treaty. The demilitarized zone between the two countries became the most heavily guarded border in the world.

An Oppressive Regime

After the Korean War, Kim remained North Korea's president, and he maintained good relationships with both China and the Soviet Union. Nevertheless, he did not want North Korea to be dominated by another

country. He vowed to make North Korea self-sufficient, and he embraced a philosophy known as *juche*, which means "self-reliance." *Juche* was more theory than reality, however. North Korea continued to depend heavily on China and the Soviets for financial support.

Kim's Communist government gave him complete control over North Korea. No one was allowed to criticize him, other political officials, or government policies. People who did so were arrested and often imprisoned. According to North Koreans

President Kim Il Sung (right) had close ties with China. He is pictured with Chinese premier Chou EnLai.

who defected (escaped) from the country, 12 prison camps were established in remote areas of North Korea, and some held as many as 150,000 people. These camps have been described as appalling, with conditions unfit for humans. People sent to these prisons had little chance of ever being released.

Kim enjoyed not only complete control, but also great luxury. He owned at least five palaces, as well as a number of other residences. Only a carefully

President Kim II Sung directed that his picture be posted in public places, such as the wall of this high school in Pyongyang.

chosen few shared his lifestyle. Uninvited guests were forbidden to visit or even set foot on the road that led to Kim's residence in Pyongyang. When he traveled, his car used special lanes, and all other traffic was banned from the road.

The "Great Leader"

Despite the fact that Kim set himself apart from the people, he had tremendous power over them. He wanted to be adored. Under his direction, thousands of monuments were built in his honor, and the main square in Pyongyang was named after him. Many universities, schools, and other institutions also bore his name.

By the 1960s, Kim's photograph was on the wall of almost every North Korean home, and all adults had to wear badges with his picture on them. He became known as the Great Leader, and people wept with joy and applauded whenever they caught a glimpse of him. This seemed strange to the few foreigners allowed to visit North Korea. They saw Kim as an oppressive leader who cared more about his lavish lifestyle than about his people. Yet, according to Don Oberdorfer, a correspondent for the *Washington Post* and an expert on Korean affairs, there was one reason why people believed their president was the greatest leader of all time: because they were forbidden to believe anything else. Oberdorfer explains: "However bizarre this belief system seems to outsiders, North Koreans are . . . instructed in it and walled off from contrary views. The great unanswered question is how many North Koreans are true believers and how many have their private doubts."[7]

In 1972, Kim met with a top South Korean leader in Seoul. This meeting, which was kept secret at first, was to discuss the possibility of reunification for the two Koreas. The leaders were cordial, and they spoke of peace and unity. No official agreement was reached, though.

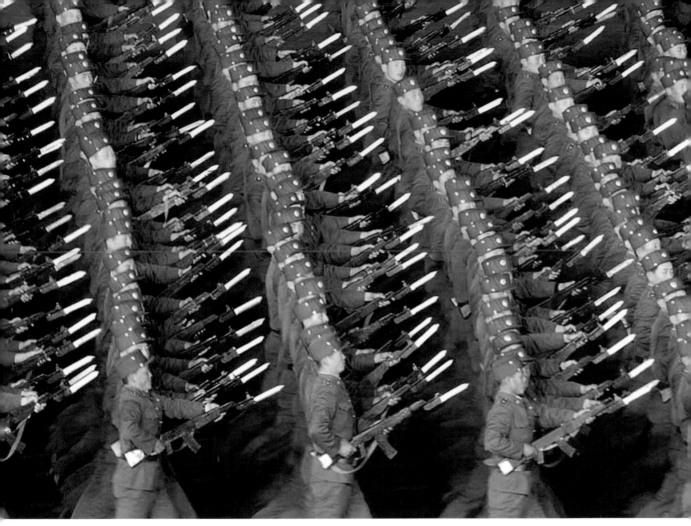

In the 1980s, North Korea had the fourth largest military in the world.

On several occasions throughout the 1970s and 1980s, officials from North and South Korea met to discuss reunification. As with the first meeting, these talks did not bring about resolutions. The relationship between the two countries remained tense and often hostile.

A Downward Spiral

During the 1980s, North Korea began to have major financial problems. It was a time of worldwide economic recession, and other countries drastically cut back on their purchases of exported products. As North

Korea's exports dropped sharply, so did its income. This meant that North Korea, which had previously borrowed a great deal of money from China, the Soviet Union, and Japan, could not pay its debts. Because those countries had financial crises of their own, they could no longer afford to help North Korea.

Another factor in North Korea's financial crunch was its military, which had become the fourth largest in the world. Despite North Korea's shortage of money, Kim maintained a large and powerful military at enormous expense.

By 1991, North Korea's economic problems were severe. The Soviet Union collapsed, and it discontinued the financial aid it had long provided to North Korea. The Soviets also stopped their export of petroleum products, which caused a steep decline in North Korea's energy supplies and fertilizer for crops. China, which hoped to improve its relationship with South Korea, did not fill the financial gap.

Although the 1990s saw continued economic decline in North Korea, relations with South Korea seemed as though they might improve. In December 1991, the two nations signed an agreement that dealt with the reunion of divided families, reestablishment of communication across the DMZ, and the free movement of people. Neither side took measures to accomplish these goals, however.

One component of the agreement was a ban on nuclear weapons. Both North and South Korea agreed not to produce, purchase, or use any type of nuclear weapon. They also signed the Nuclear Safeguards Agreement, which allowed for international inspection of nuclear facilities. A year and a half later, however, North Korea formally withdrew from the Nuclear Nonproliferation Treaty, an international pact designed to limit the spread of nuclear weapons. North Korea later canceled this withdrawal, but it had caused fear in South Korea and throughout the world that it was secretly developing nuclear weapons.

In July 1994, Kim made a surprise announcement—that he intended to freeze North Korea's nuclear program and would meet with South Korea's president to resume peace talks. Both leaders hoped they could finally arrive at a reunification agreement. The meeting never happened, however. As Kim prepared for his visitor's arrival, he suffered a massive heart attack and died.

After Kim's death, his son, Kim Jong Il, became commander of the country's armed forces. Four years later, he became head of North Korea's Communist Party. He led the government and was called the Dear Leader, but he could not officially become president. That title was eternally assigned to his deceased father. In fact, a common belief among North Koreans was that Kim Il Sung would rule forever from the grave.

Kim Jong Il, son of Kim Il Sung, became the leader of North Korea when his father died.

WHAT IS COMMUNISM?

Kim Jong Il, North Korea's leader, has total control over the people. They have no freedom of speech, no freedom of religion, and no freedom to choose how to live their lives. North Korea is a Communist country, and many people believe that the type of oppression seen in North Korea is what defines communism. The original intent of communism, however, was something very different. When the concept was first developed, its intent was to benefit people—not to hurt them or take away their freedom.

Karl Marx, a German intellectual who lived during the 1800s, first developed the idea of communism. He was dismayed by class differences between wealthy property owners (capitalists) and common workers (the proletariat). His idea was to create equality among people and to eliminate societies in which only a privileged few had all the wealth. Marx believed that society would benefit if wealth were distributed more

equally, according to people's abilities and needs. He also thought that if the government were in charge of the economy and property, a country was more likely to prosper. This, he believed, would be of great benefit to the people.

Marx wrote extensively about communism. His writings later became the foundation that political leaders, including Vladimir Lenin of Russia and Mao Tse-tung of China, used to form their own Communist governments. The societies created by Lenin, Mao, and other Communist leaders were not what Marx had envisioned, however. They were strict and dictatorial. People had no individual freedoms, and the government controlled not just the economy, but almost every aspect of the people's lives. The press was censored and was not allowed to print news stories that criticized the government. Religion was either controlled or banned altogether. People could not own property, and those who spoke out against the

German intellectual Karl Marx was dismayed with class differences. This led him to develop the idea of communism.

government were punished, and sometimes imprisoned or killed.

Communism spread throughout the world, and by the mid-1900s, many countries had adopted it. Over time, however, it became apparent that communism did not lead to prosperity at all. In fact, it often left nations poverty-stricken. By 1990, Poland, East Germany, Czechoslovakia, Bulgaria, Romania, and Hungary had all abandoned their Communist governments. In 1991, the Soviet Union dissolved, and was no longer a Communist nation. Today, only five Communist countries remain in the world: China, Vietnam, Cuba, Laos, and North Korea.

CHAPTER THREE
An Uncertain Future

In the years since Kim Jong Il became the leader of North Korea, conditions in the country have continued to grow worse. North Korea has received more than one billion dollars in aid from international relief organizations, including tons of food and medical supplies—yet the country's people remain undernourished, and many have died of starvation. Vollertsen says that international agencies must turn over all supplies and financial aid to the North Korean government, which is in charge of distribution. The country's military is still the government's first priority. The rest of the people receive only what is left over. Vollertsen explains: "The system's beneficiaries are members of the Communist Party and high-ranking military personnel. In Pyongyang, these people enjoy a comfortable lifestyle. . . . In the countryside, starving people, bypassed by the aid intended for them, forage for food."[8]

Harsh Realities

In addition to mass starvation, the people suffer many other hardships. There is a lack of fuel, so homes, schools, and hospitals are often unheated. Much of the country's water is contaminated because insufficient fuel

Many international relief organizations, including the Red Cross, have sent food and medical supplies to North Korea.

has caused water treatment plants to break down. The people are also weak from undernourishment, which makes them vulnerable to disease. Malaria, for example, afflicted 100,000 North Koreans in 2000.

The North Korean government attempts to hide the country's problems from foreigners. Few visitors are allowed to travel outside of Pyongyang, so they are not often aware of how grim conditions are in other areas. The rare visitors who have traveled throughout North Korea say that the people are victims of a cruel regime that completely controls their lives. Telephones are tapped and people are constantly watched. Radios and televisions receive only official government channels. People are forced to perform manual labor, and children as young as eight years old are required to work on roads, breaking up rocks with hammers.

The North Korean people also endure terrible health care conditions. Most hospitals are dirty and unsanitary, and have no heat, clean bandages, or medicines. Equipment is crude. In stark contrast, the hospitals that treat higher-class people, such as members of the Communist Party and the military, are modern, clean, and equipped with the latest medical instruments and supplies. Vollertsen explains: "There are two worlds in North Korea, one for the senior military and the elite; and a living hell for the rest."[9]

Weapons of Mass Destruction

Just as the North Korean government is secretive about the plight of its people, it also tightly controls information about the weapons it possesses. In 1996, a high-ranking North Korean official named Hwang Jang-yop defected from the country. He revealed that North Korea had nuclear weapons and planned to conduct an underground test—the last stage in a full nuclear weapons program. In 1998, spy satellite pictures revealed the underground site, which was attended by thousands of workers.

In 2002, South Koreans in Seoul protested North Korea's nuclear weapons program.

THE MOST DANGEROUS WEAPONS ON EARTH

In the aftermath of the September 11, 2001, attacks on the United States, President George W. Bush gave a speech about terrorism. He used the term "Axis of Evil" in reference to three countries: Iraq, Iran, and North Korea. One reason Bush chose that term is because each of these countries has developed weapons of mass destruction (WMD).

All weapons are dangerous, but WMD are especially deadly. Their purpose is to cause extremely widespread damage, injury, and death. The effects of these weapons cannot be predicted or controlled, and they can kill thousands of people in an instant.

One example of a very powerful—and deadly—type of WMD is the nuclear bomb. When nuclear bombs explode, they create a wave of intense heat. The temperature is so high, in fact, that objects near the center of the blast can actually be vaporized. That means the heat from the bomb can make objects—

and living things—disappear entirely. Even people who are not close to a nuclear bomb blast are likely to suffer serious burns or long-term health problems caused by the bomb's radioactive particles.

Chemical and biological weapons are another form of WMD. They can be used to release toxic substances, called agents. These agents can be spread through the air, through contaminated food and water supplies, or through direct human contact. The most effective way for these agents to be spread is by emission into the air, either by an exploding bomb or some type of spray mechanism.

Chemical weapons spread poisonous chemical substances. Nerve agents, mustard agents, and tear gas are examples of chemical agents. These poisons attack the body's nerves, blood, skin, or lungs. Certain effects, such as tears, vomiting, or blistering of the skin, may be temporary. Some effects,

Nuclear bombs are one type of weapon of mass destruction. When one explodes, heat and debris rise into the air. This causes a giant mushroom cloud to form.

however, may be permanent, such as paralysis or even death.

Biological weapons spread infectious bacteria or viruses. These weapons can spread deadly diseases such as bubonic plague, smallpox, and hepatitis. Another disease that can be spread by biological weapons is anthrax. In its natural form, anthrax usually attacks hoofed animals, such as cattle, sheep, and horses. It can, however, be produced in laboratories and used to infect humans. Because anthrax almost always causes death when it is inhaled, it is considered the most dangerous biological agent of all.

When this discovery was made, Henry Sokolski, who heads an organization called the Nonproliferation Policy Education Center, predicted that North Korea will be able to produce large numbers of nuclear weapons in the future: "They have uranium [a chemical element used in nuclear weapons] mines all over the place. Once they get this process going, there are going to be big problems."[10]

Suspicions about North Korea's nuclear weapons were confirmed in October 2002. A U.S. official visited Pyongyang to meet with one of Kim Jong Il's top aides. During the meeting, the North Korean representative admitted that his country did indeed have a nuclear weapons program. He said that since U.S. president George W. Bush had referred to his country as one of the "Axis of Evil" nations (along with Iran and Iraq), North Korea might become a target of U.S. aggression. He claimed the country needed nuclear weapons to defend itself.

This revelation precipitated an international crisis that escalated in the months that followed. In December, North Korea reactivated its Yongbyon nuclear power plant, which had been shut down since 1994. Later that month, North Korean leaders demanded that the UN's watchdog International Atomic Energy Agency remove its seals and surveillance equipment from the plant. On December 21, North Korea dismantled the monitoring devices, and in January 2003, officially withdrew from the Nuclear Nonproliferation Treaty.

Nuclear weapons are not the only threat posed by North Korea. Another fact revealed in the October 2002 meeting was that the country has other powerful weapons, most likely chemical and biological weapons. Hwang had also warned about these weapons. In fact, he said that North Korea had a huge arsenal of weapons, which included a variety of deadly poisons. A report by the U.S. Department of State

The construction of this nuclear reactor in North Korea, shown here in a satellite photo, was halted in 1994 as part of an arms control agreement with the United States.

confirmed that North Korea had stockpiled several chemical agents and also had the ability to produce biological weapons, including anthrax, smallpox, and bacteria that cause deadly diseases such as cholera and the plague.

What Will Happen Next?

No one knows for sure what the future holds for North Korea. The country's reopening of the Yongbyon power plant has sparked world-wide fears that North Korea is attempting to make nuclear bombs. Even worse, experts theorize that North Korea might be willing to sell materials for making nuclear weapons to countries that support terrorism.

Although weapons issues have focused international attention on North Korea, little has changed for the nation's people. North Korea is still a society in which ordinary citizens have no freedom or control over their own lives. The health care system serves the country's elite, while common people die of disease. Government leaders live in luxury and spend millions of dollars on ceremonies and monuments, but thousands of North Koreans go hungry. No reunification agreement has been reached with South Korea, so families are still separated. In many cases, family members on opposite sides of the DMZ have never even met.

North Korea's weapons of mass destruction pose a grave threat to South Korea, as well as to other countries. Vollertsen believes that the North Korean people can only be saved if the rest of the world pressures the government to change. He explains: "The people can't help themselves. They are brainwashed, and too afraid to be able to overthrow their rulers."[11]

In 2000, North Korean leader Jon Kum-jin (second from right) met with South Korean leader Park Jae-kyu (second from left) to discuss ways to ease tension between the two nations.

In January 2003, North Koreans who fled to South Korea released white doves in the demilitarized zone to symbolize their hope for peace.

Whether Korea will ever again be a unified country whose people are free from oppression is unknown. The people of North Korea have suffered more than almost any nation on earth. Still, despite all the hardships they have endured, they somehow manage to go on. McCune sees hope for the future: "Friends of Korea . . . must take solace [comfort] in the abiding nature of this land of high mountains and sparkling streams, in the enduring qualities of mind and spirit possessed by the Korean people, and in the hope that some peaceful morning the calm, now broken, will be restored."[12]

Important Dates

2333 B.C.	According to Korean legend, the kingdom of Choson is founded by a man named Tangun.
108 B.C.	China conquers Choson and establishes four colonies.
A.D. **313**	The Chosons overthrow the Chinese, reclaim their land, and establish the Three Kingdoms: Koguryo, Paekche, and Silla.
668	Sillas conquer the other two kingdoms and unify Korea as one country.
935	Wang Kon, a Korean general, seizes control from the Sillas.
1231	Mongol forces invade Korea.
1392	Yi Song-gye, a Korean general, joins forces with the Chinese Ming Dynasty and seizes control of Korea.
1592–1636	Japanese and Manchurians attempt to invade Korea on several occasions.
Early 1800s	Leaders of the Yi Dynasty close the country to non-Chinese foreigners.
1876	Japan uses military force to pressure Korea to reestablish commercial trade; Korea also establishes trade agreements with the United States and European countries.
1910	Japan assumes control over Korea and makes it a Japanese colony.
1919	The March First Movement takes place in Korea; Declaration of Independence is signed; Japanese respond with brutal force.
1943	United States, Great Britain, and China sign the Cairo Declaration, which promises freedom to the people of Korea.
1945	Japan surrenders to the United States, ending World War II; Japan loses control of Korea.
1948	Korea is permanently divided into two nations: the Republic of Korea (South Korea) and the Democratic People's Republic of Korea (North Korea).
1950	North Korean president Kim Il Sung launches surprise invasion of South Korea, which starts the Korean War.

1953	North Korea, China, and UN representatives sign an armistice to bring an end to the war.
1972	Leaders from North and South Korea meet to discuss peace and reunification.
1991	North and South Korea sign the Nuclear Safeguards Agreement, which bans production of nuclear weapons.
1993	North Korea formally withdraws from the Nuclear Nonproliferation Treaty, an international pact designed to limit the spread of nuclear weapons; the country later cancels the withdrawal.
1994	Kim announces that he intends to freeze North Korea's nuclear program and resume peace talks with South Korea; he dies; his son, Kim Jong Il, becomes the North Korean leader.
1996	High-ranking official Hwang Jang-yop defects from North Korea; he reveals that the country has nuclear, biological, and chemical weapons.
1998	Spy satellite photographs reveal an underground nuclear weapons production facility in North Korea.
2002	In a meeting with a U.S. official, North Korea admits that it has a nuclear weapons program.

About the Author

Peggy J. Parks holds a Bachelor of Science degree from Aquinas College in Grand Rapids, Michigan, where she graduated magna cum laude. She is a freelance writer who has written numerous titles for The Gale Group, including the Lucent Books Careers for the 21st Century series, the Blackbirch Press Giants of Science and Nations in Crisis series, and the KidHaven Press Exploring Careers series. She was previously the profile writer for *Grand Rapids: The City That Works*, produced by Towery Publications. Parks lives in Muskegon, Michigan, a town that she says inspires her writing because of its location on the shores of Lake Michigan.

For More Information

BOOKS

Elaine Landau, *Korea*. New York: Childrens Press, 1999.

Sylvia McNair, *Korea*. Chicago: Childrens Press, 1986.

Frances Park and Ginger Park, *My Freedom Trip: A Child's Escape from North Korea*. Honesdale, PA: Boyds Mill Press, 1998.

PERIODICALS

Sara Hammes and Steven Manning, "Can the Koreas Unite?" *Scholastic Update*, March 20, 1992. An article about North and South Korea's reunification efforts.

Howard Hwang, "Koreans Have Mixed Emotions About Possible Reunification," *LA Youth*, September/October 2000, p. 10. A 14-year-old Korean boy shares his thoughts on the reunification of North and South Korea.

Lee Kravitz, "Rogue Nation," *Current Events*, November 5, 1999. An article about the differences between North and South Korea, including how the countries became divided.

_____, "Winds of Change," *Scholastic Update,* March 20, 1992. An article about the peace talks between North and South Korea.

WEBSITES

CIA World Factbook
This official CIA website offers maps, facts, and up-to-date information on North Korea.
www.cia.gov/cia/publications/factbook/geos/kn.html

Infoplease.com
This website includes information on the history, geography, and people of North Korea.
www.infoplease.com/ipa/A0107686.html

Lonely Planet World Guide—North Korea
An informative website that focuses on traveling to North Korea.
www.lonelyplanet.com/destinations/north_east_asia/north_korea

Source Quotations

1. Shannon McCune, *Korea: Land of Broken Calm*, Princeton, NJ: Van Nostrand, 1966, p. 1.

2. Ellie Kuykendall, interview with author, October 15, 2002.

3. Norbert Vollertsen, "A Prison Country," *Wall Street Journal* editorial page, April 17, 2001.

4. Vollertsen, "A Prison Country."

5. Kuykendall, interview with author.

6. Quoted in "Cairo Conference 1943," The Avalon Project at Yale Law School. www.yale.edu/lawweb/avalon/wwii/cairo.htm.

7. Don Oberdorfer, *The Two Koreas,* Reading, MA: Addison-Wesley, 1997, p. 20.

8. Vollertsen, "A Prison Country."

9. Vollertsen, "A Prison Country."

10. Quoted in Bill Gertz, "U.S. Saw North Korea's Work to Enrich Fuel for Nukes," *Washington Times,* October 18, 2002. www.washtimes.com/national/20021018=82935839.htm

11. Vollertsen, "A Prison Country."

12. McCune, *Korea: Land of Broken Calm*, p. 209.

Index